Just Write Bitch!

a journal for badass lady bosses

Just Write Bitch! is a work of my own creation.

This journal does not replace the advice of a medical professional or trained therapist. Consult your physician before making any changes to your diet or regular health plan.

And for God's sake, please, utilize common sense, not only in the reading of this book, but in all areas of your life.

The information in this book was correct at the time of publication, and the Author does not assume any liability for loss or damage caused by errors or omissions, again, this is my perspective, opinion, and experience, so it has been written as such.

ISBN - 979-8-9865393-0-0

Cover, Book Design, and Layout by Megs Thompson
www.megswrites.com

in omnia paratus Publishing

Hello Gorgeous!

Whether you're a notebook hoarder, an avid writer, or a journal-virgin, this journal was created for you!

Filled with 111 eclectic, no-nonsense, thought-provoking prompts inviting you to write creatively, honestly, and sometimes uncomfortably - warming up your writing muscles & getting the creative juices flowing.

How much or little you write for each prompt is entirely up to you - however, I do recommend setting a timer for 15 minutes when you're first getting started.

There is no right or wrong way to use these pages & prompts. Go in order, skip around, close your eyes and pick a page at random - it's really up to you..

I've made sure to include a handful of extra pages at the back of the journal that can be torn out & used for any prompts where more space is needed, or for jotting down to-do & shopping lists if you'd rather.

With that - there's only one thing left to do...

Just Write Bitch!

Spend a few moments observing a stranger - from a safe distance. Who are they? What's their story?
Have fun with this but whatever you do, do NOT follow them to their panel van.

_____

_____

_____

_____

_____

_____

_____

_____

_____

_____

_____

_____

_____

_____

_____

_____

_____

_____

_____

_____

_____

_____

_____

_____

_____

Just Write Bitch!

As a child, what did you dream of doing when you grew up?
Why? Do you still have that dream? If not, when did it
change?

_____

_____

_____

_____

_____

_____

_____

_____

_____

_____

_____

_____

_____

_____

_____

_____

_____

_____

_____

_____

_____

_____

_____

_____

_____

_____

_____

_____

Just Write Bitch!

Who is one person you trust fully. How long have you known them? What role do they play in your life? What is it about them that makes you trust them?

_____
_____
_____
_____
_____
_____
_____
_____
_____
_____
_____
_____
_____
_____
_____
_____
_____
_____
_____
_____
_____
_____
_____
_____
_____

Just Write Bitch!

If you could create one law or regulation that had to be followed by everyone on Earth, what would it be? How would you enforce it? Would there be repercussions for those who broke the law?

_____
_____
_____
_____
_____
_____
_____
_____
_____
_____
_____
_____
_____
_____
_____
_____
_____
_____
_____
_____
_____
_____
_____
_____
_____
_____
_____
_____

Just Write Bitch!

What quirk or behavior bothers you most? Maybe it's
chewing gum, belching, or saying 'like' too much. When did
you first notice this bothered you?

_____
_____
_____
_____
_____
_____
_____
_____
_____
_____
_____
_____
_____
_____
_____
_____
_____
_____
_____
_____
_____
_____
_____
_____
_____
_____
_____

Just Write Bitch!

Close your eyes and imagine, what color do you feel like today? Why?

_____

_____

_____

_____

_____

_____

_____

_____

_____

_____

_____

_____

_____

_____

_____

_____

_____

_____

_____

_____

_____

_____

_____

_____

_____

Just Write Bitch!

Write a letter to your future self.

Just Write Bitch!

Write about an incredibly difficult choice you've had to make
and how it's affected your life.

_____

_____

_____

_____

_____

_____

_____

_____

_____

_____

_____

_____

_____

_____

_____

_____

_____

_____

_____

_____

_____

_____

_____

_____

_____

_____

_____

Just Write Bitch!

What are 3 ways that your personality has changed since childhood? What are three ways that it's the same?

_____
_____
_____
_____
_____
_____
_____
_____
_____
_____
_____
_____
_____
_____
_____
_____
_____
_____
_____
_____
_____
_____
_____
_____
_____
_____

Just Write Bitch!

What was your last unexplainable experience? Something that gave you pause, left you shaken, and questioning - 'did that actually happen?'

_____
_____
_____
_____
_____
_____
_____
_____
_____
_____
_____
_____
_____
_____
_____
_____
_____
_____
_____
_____
_____
_____
_____
_____
_____
_____

Just Write Bitch!

What do you remember most about the kitchen in your childhood home? Is it a smell, a taste, an object, a feeling?

_____
_____
_____
_____
_____
_____
_____
_____
_____
_____
_____
_____
_____
_____
_____
_____
_____
_____
_____
_____
_____
_____
_____
_____
_____
_____
_____

Just Write Bitch!

What would you do if you knew you couldn't fail?

Just Write Bitch!

What's the biggest risk you've ever taken? Was the result anything like you'd hoped?

_____

_____

_____

_____

_____

_____

_____

_____

_____

_____

_____

_____

_____

_____

_____

_____

_____

_____

_____

_____

_____

_____

_____

_____

_____

Just Write Bitch!

What impression do you want to leave on those you interact with? Does this differ in your personal & professional life?

_____
_____
_____
_____
_____
_____
_____
_____
_____
_____
_____
_____
_____
_____
_____
_____
_____
_____
_____
_____
_____
_____
_____
_____
_____
_____

Just Write Bitch!

Think of someone in your life, past or present, that you'd like to tell how you *really* feel. This may be good or bad, loving or hateful. Write them a letter.

_____

_____

_____

_____

_____

_____

_____

_____

_____

_____

_____

_____

_____

_____

_____

_____

_____

_____

_____

_____

_____

_____

_____

_____

_____

_____

_____

Just Write Bitch!

Take a moment to look around you. What aspects of your current surroundings make you feel most comfortable & safe?

_____
_____
_____
_____
_____
_____
_____
_____
_____
_____
_____
_____
_____
_____
_____
_____
_____
_____
_____
_____
_____
_____
_____

Just Write Bitch!

How would you describe your personal culture? This may include practices and beliefs from your childhood, your heritage, your community, or rituals you've created for yourself.

Just Write Bitch!

What are 3 challenges you've overcome? What lessons have you learned? How has the accomplishment changed your life?

_____
_____
_____
_____
_____
_____
_____
_____
_____
_____
_____
_____
_____
_____
_____
_____
_____
_____
_____
_____
_____
_____
_____
_____
_____
_____
_____

Just Write Bitch!

Do you have a favorite season? What is it about that time of year that you enjoy the most? Have you experienced that season in another place, climate?

_____
_____
_____
_____
_____
_____
_____
_____
_____
_____
_____
_____
_____
_____
_____
_____
_____
_____
_____
_____
_____
_____
_____
_____
_____

Just Write Bitch!

When was the last time you observed a moment of selfless compassion? Describe the situation, the people, the actions you witnessed. Do you know what was happening or are you making assumptions? Assume away!

_____
_____
_____
_____
_____
_____
_____
_____
_____
_____
_____
_____
_____
_____
_____
_____
_____
_____
_____
_____
_____
_____
_____
_____
_____
_____
_____
_____

Just Write Bitch!

If you had an imaginary friend now, as an adult, what would they look like? What's their name? Are they your age, older, or younger? What would you do together? What would you talk about?

_____
_____
_____
_____
_____
_____
_____
_____
_____
_____
_____
_____
_____
_____
_____
_____
_____
_____
_____
_____
_____
_____
_____
_____
_____
_____
_____
_____
_____

Just Write Bitch!

Do you remember having a favorite piece of furniture in your childhood home? What was it? What made it stand out to you?

_____
_____
_____
_____
_____
_____
_____
_____
_____
_____
_____
_____
_____
_____
_____
_____
_____
_____
_____
_____
_____
_____
_____
_____
_____

Just Write Bitch!

When do you trust yourself most?

_____
_____
_____
_____
_____
_____
_____
_____
_____
_____
_____
_____
_____
_____
_____
_____
_____
_____
_____
_____
_____
_____
_____
_____
_____
_____
_____

Just Write Bitch!

What are 5 things you'd like your loved ones, potential friends, and partners, to know about you?

_____
_____
_____
_____
_____
_____
_____
_____
_____
_____
_____
_____
_____
_____
_____
_____
_____
_____
_____
_____
_____
_____
_____
_____
_____
_____
_____
_____

Just Write Bitch!

How do you show yourself kindness and compassion each day?

_____

_____

_____

_____

_____

_____

_____

_____

_____

_____

_____

_____

_____

_____

_____

_____

_____

_____

_____

_____

_____

_____

Just Write Bitch!

Describe in detail the worst date experience you've had.
What made it bad? Where was it? How did it smell? Who was
your date?

_____
_____
_____
_____
_____
_____
_____
_____
_____
_____
_____
_____
_____
_____
_____
_____
_____
_____
_____
_____
_____
_____
_____
_____
_____

Just Write Bitch!

What are your thoughts on ghosts, spirits, and the supernatural? Have you ever had an experience you couldn't explain?

_____
_____
_____
_____
_____
_____
_____
_____
_____
_____
_____
_____
_____
_____
_____
_____
_____
_____
_____
_____
_____
_____
_____
_____
_____
_____
_____
_____

Just Write Bitch!

Think of a location, someplace unfamiliar, that piques your curiosity. What is it that attracts you? Why haven't you explored the location? What secrets might the location hold?

_____
_____
_____
_____
_____
_____
_____
_____
_____
_____
_____
_____
_____
_____
_____
_____
_____
_____
_____
_____
_____
_____
_____
_____
_____
_____

Just Write Bitch!

How has your identity changed over the course of your life?

Just Write Bitch!

Reflect on a small, seemingly boring moment that happened today. Write about it in as much detail as possible, using each of your senses.

_____
_____
_____
_____
_____
_____
_____
_____
_____
_____
_____
_____
_____
_____
_____
_____
_____
_____
_____
_____
_____
_____
_____
_____
_____
_____

Just Write Bitch!

Growing up, what was your favorite celebration? What was it about this holiday or event that you enjoyed most? Has this changed as you've aged?

_____

_____

_____

_____

_____

_____

_____

_____

_____

_____

_____

_____

_____

_____

_____

_____

_____

_____

_____

_____

_____

_____

_____

_____

Just Write Bitch!

Write a letter to your past self.

Just Write Bitch!

What are 5 skills or areas of expertise that you possess that make you unique? How did you learn or develop these skills? How do they factor into your daily life?

_____
_____
_____
_____
_____
_____
_____
_____
_____
_____
_____
_____
_____
_____
_____
_____
_____
_____
_____
_____
_____
_____
_____
_____
_____
_____

Just Write Bitch!

What legends or crazy stories do you remember hearing about your hometown growing up? Maybe it was an abandoned mine, a haunted bell tower, or a crazed cat lady who wanders the streets at night searching for her next pet?

_____

_____

_____

_____

_____

_____

_____

_____

_____

_____

_____

_____

_____

_____

_____

_____

_____

_____

_____

_____

_____

_____

_____

_____

Just Write Bitch!

What do you remember most about your bedroom as a
child? Is it a smell, an object, a feeling, an experience?

_____

_____

_____

_____

_____

_____

_____

_____

_____

_____

_____

_____

_____

_____

_____

_____

_____

_____

_____

_____

_____

_____

_____

_____

_____

Just Write Bitch!

Write a letter of forgiveness to someone else.

Just Write Bitch!

What would you do if you could live a single day without any
consequences for your actions?

_____
_____
_____
_____
_____
_____
_____
_____
_____
_____
_____
_____
_____
_____
_____
_____
_____
_____
_____
_____
_____
_____
_____
_____
_____

Just Write Bitch!

What legacy do you want to leave behind? What are you
doing today to make that happen?

_____
_____
_____
_____
_____
_____
_____
_____
_____
_____
_____
_____
_____
_____
_____
_____
_____
_____
_____
_____
_____
_____
_____
_____
_____
_____
_____

Just Write Bitch!

If you were given the choice between being ridiculously famous & successful or living happily ever after with your soulmate in a shack, which would you choose & why?

_____
_____
_____
_____
_____
_____
_____
_____
_____
_____
_____
_____
_____
_____
_____
_____
_____
_____
_____
_____
_____
_____
_____
_____
_____
_____

Just Write Bitch!

When was the last time you experienced a failure that turned out to be a blessing? What changed, the situation or your perception?

_____
_____
_____
_____
_____
_____
_____
_____
_____
_____
_____
_____
_____
_____
_____
_____
_____
_____
_____
_____
_____
_____
_____
_____
_____
_____
_____

Just Write Bitch!

Think of someone in your life that you'd like to break up
with. It may be a family member, a coworker, or an overly-
chatty neighbor. Write them a letter. Be brutally honest -
trust me - it feels amazing!

_____

_____

_____

_____

_____

_____

_____

_____

_____

_____

_____

_____

_____

_____

_____

_____

_____

_____

_____

_____

_____

_____

_____

_____

_____

_____

Just Write Bitch!

Do you have a mantra or affirmation that you use regularly?
What is it? What does it mean to you? If not, now's a great
time to find one or write your own!

_____
_____
_____
_____
_____
_____
_____
_____
_____
_____
_____
_____
_____
_____
_____
_____
_____
_____
_____
_____
_____
_____
_____
_____

Just Write Bitch!

What assumptions do people make about you? Are they true?
How does this make you feel?

_____
_____
_____
_____
_____
_____
_____
_____
_____
_____
_____
_____
_____
_____
_____
_____
_____
_____
_____
_____
_____
_____
_____
_____
_____

Just Write Bitch!

What do you remember most about your parents growing up?

_____

_____

_____

_____

_____

_____

_____

_____

_____

_____

_____

_____

_____

_____

_____

_____

_____

_____

_____

_____

_____

_____

_____

_____

_____

_____

Just Write Bitch!

What does your perfect Sunday look like? Where are you?
Who are you with? What are you doing? What kind of
weather?

_____
_____
_____
_____
_____
_____
_____
_____
_____
_____
_____
_____
_____
_____
_____
_____
_____
_____
_____
_____
_____
_____
_____
_____

Just Write Bitch!

When was the last time you experienced deja vu?

_____
_____
_____
_____
_____
_____
_____
_____
_____
_____
_____
_____
_____
_____
_____
_____
_____
_____
_____
_____
_____
_____
_____
_____
_____

Just Write Bitch!

Have you ever crossed paths with someone who captured your attention, only to lose touch or fail to make a connection? Write about a 'missed connection' you wish went differently.

_____

_____

_____

_____

_____

_____

_____

_____

_____

_____

_____

_____

_____

_____

_____

_____

_____

_____

_____

_____

_____

_____

_____

_____

Just Write Bitch!

What is one moment that you use to divide your life into a before and after? This may be something big, like a national disaster, or something personal, like a private loss. It may be positive or negative.

_____
_____
_____
_____
_____
_____
_____
_____
_____
_____
_____
_____
_____
_____
_____
_____
_____
_____
_____
_____
_____
_____
_____
_____
_____
_____

Just Write Bitch!

What are 3 small things in your daily life that bring you pleasure? What is it about them? What does that pleasure feel like - is it different for each one?

_____
_____
_____
_____
_____
_____
_____
_____
_____
_____
_____
_____
_____
_____
_____
_____
_____
_____
_____
_____
_____
_____
_____
_____
_____

Just Write Bitch!

Write your own eulogy - how do you want to be
remembered?

_____
_____
_____
_____
_____
_____
_____
_____
_____
_____
_____
_____
_____
_____
_____
_____
_____
_____
_____
_____
_____
_____
_____
_____
_____

Just Write Bitch!

Write a love letter to yourself.

_____
_____
_____
_____
_____
_____
_____
_____
_____
_____
_____
_____
_____
_____
_____
_____
_____
_____
_____
_____
_____
_____
_____
_____
_____

Just Write Bitch!

What are 3 of your favorite smells? Describe, in detail, how each of them makes you feel. What do they remind you of?

_____
_____
_____
_____
_____
_____
_____
_____
_____
_____
_____
_____
_____
_____
_____
_____
_____
_____
_____
_____
_____
_____
_____
_____
_____
_____
_____

Just Write Bitch!

When was the last time you laughed so hard you cried? What was so funny?

_____
_____
_____
_____
_____
_____
_____
_____
_____
_____
_____
_____
_____
_____
_____
_____
_____
_____
_____
_____
_____
_____
_____
_____

Just Write Bitch!

Describe yourself as you might exist on the other side of a
mirror - as the opposite of your current self.

_____
_____
_____
_____
_____
_____
_____
_____
_____
_____
_____
_____
_____
_____
_____
_____
_____
_____
_____
_____
_____
_____
_____
_____
_____

Just Write Bitch!

What does passion mean to you? What does it look like, feel like, sound like, smell like?

_____

_____

_____

_____

_____

_____

_____

_____

_____

_____

_____

_____

_____

_____

_____

_____

_____

_____

_____

_____

_____

_____

_____

_____

_____

Just Write Bitch!

When your house is completely silent, how does it feel? Are you comfortable in the silence? Why or why not?

_____
_____
_____
_____
_____
_____
_____
_____
_____
_____
_____
_____
_____
_____
_____
_____
_____
_____
_____
_____
_____
_____
_____

Just Write Bitch!

Reflect back to your youth. What outlandish assumptions did you have about the adults in your life?

_____
_____
_____
_____
_____
_____
_____
_____
_____
_____
_____
_____
_____
_____
_____
_____
_____
_____
_____
_____
_____
_____
_____
_____
_____

Just Write Bitch!

We all have memorable family members, some more eccentric than others. What are some of the more unique characteristics you recognize with your family. How have they affected holiday gatherings?

_____
_____
_____
_____
_____
_____
_____
_____
_____
_____
_____
_____
_____
_____
_____
_____
_____
_____
_____
_____
_____
_____
_____
_____
_____
_____

Just Write Bitch!

What achievements do you dream of accomplishing in life?
What actions are you taking to make this happen?

_____
_____
_____
_____
_____
_____
_____
_____
_____
_____
_____
_____
_____
_____
_____
_____
_____
_____
_____
_____
_____
_____
_____
_____
_____

Just Write Bitch!

What are 3 pieces of advice you wish you could share with
your teenage self?

_____

_____

_____

_____

_____

_____

_____

_____

_____

_____

_____

_____

_____

_____

_____

_____

_____

_____

_____

_____

_____

_____

_____

_____

_____

_____

Just Write Bitch!

What parts of your life have surprised you the most? Are there specific things that have turned out differently than you would have expected or had planned?

_____
_____
_____
_____
_____
_____
_____
_____
_____
_____
_____
_____
_____
_____
_____
_____
_____
_____
_____
_____
_____
_____
_____
_____
_____
_____

Just Write Bitch!

What habits or lessons do you most want your children (or
future children) to learn from you?

Just Write Bitch!

What was the last strong emotion you experienced? What brought up that emotion and feeling? Was it positive or negative?

_____
_____
_____
_____
_____
_____
_____
_____
_____
_____
_____
_____
_____
_____
_____
_____
_____
_____
_____
_____
_____
_____
_____
_____
_____
_____

Just Write Bitch!

Imagine seeing yourself from the perspective of a bug.
Describe what they see.

Just Write Bitch!

What are 3 things that can instantly disrupt a good mood
and bring you down? What strategies do you use to counter
these effects?

_____
_____
_____
_____
_____
_____
_____
_____
_____
_____
_____
_____
_____
_____
_____
_____
_____
_____
_____
_____
_____
_____
_____
_____
_____

Just Write Bitch!

When do you find it most difficult to have faith and trust your instincts?

_____

_____

_____

_____

_____

_____

_____

_____

_____

_____

_____

_____

_____

_____

_____

_____

_____

_____

_____

_____

_____

_____

_____

_____

_____

_____

_____

Just Write Bitch!

You've landed your dream job, searching for mythical beasts. Are you chasing Sasquatch, Yeti, Chupacabra, Mothman, Aliens, or something else? What does a Monday look like for you?

_____

_____

_____

_____

_____

_____

_____

_____

_____

_____

_____

_____

_____

_____

_____

_____

_____

_____

_____

_____

_____

_____

_____

_____

_____

_____

_____

Just Write Bitch!

When was the last time you experienced the kindness of a
stranger? Describe the interaction & how you felt.

Just Write Bitch!

What's been the best year of your life so far? How old were you? What made it so memorably amazing? What was happening in the world around you - near & far?

_____
_____
_____
_____
_____
_____
_____
_____
_____
_____
_____
_____
_____
_____
_____
_____
_____
_____
_____
_____
_____
_____
_____
_____
_____

Just Write Bitch!

Describe a day in the life of your favorite pet, from their point of view. What do they think about? What do they worry about? What do they do when left to their own devices?

_____
_____
_____
_____
_____
_____
_____
_____
_____
_____
_____
_____
_____
_____
_____
_____
_____
_____
_____
_____
_____
_____
_____
_____
_____

Just Write Bitch!

What are 3 personal beliefs you hold? Are these non-negotiables for you, or beliefs you're still exploring & forming? How have these beliefs been influenced by others?

_____

_____

_____

_____

_____

_____

_____

_____

_____

_____

_____

_____

_____

_____

_____

_____

_____

_____

_____

_____

_____

_____

_____

_____

_____

Just Write Bitch!

What aspects of your life are you most grateful for?

_____
_____
_____
_____
_____
_____
_____
_____
_____
_____
_____
_____
_____
_____
_____
_____
_____
_____
_____
_____
_____
_____
_____
_____
_____
_____

Just Write Bitch!

Describe an important memory from your childhood from the perspective of someone else who was present. How does their recollection differ from your own?

_____
_____
_____
_____
_____
_____
_____
_____
_____
_____
_____
_____
_____
_____
_____
_____
_____
_____
_____
_____
_____
_____
_____
_____
_____
_____
_____

Just Write Bitch!

What does true love mean to you?

_____
_____
_____
_____
_____
_____
_____
_____
_____
_____
_____
_____
_____
_____
_____
_____
_____
_____
_____
_____
_____
_____
_____
_____
_____
_____

Just Write Bitch!

Do your current goals accurately reflect your personal desires, or those of someone else? If they belong to someone else, how does that make you feel?

_____
_____
_____
_____
_____
_____
_____
_____
_____
_____
_____
_____
_____
_____
_____
_____
_____
_____
_____
_____
_____
_____
_____
_____
_____

Just Write Bitch!

What is one secret that you've never shared with anyone, but wish you could share with the person you love most?

_____
_____
_____
_____
_____
_____
_____
_____
_____
_____
_____
_____
_____
_____
_____
_____
_____
_____
_____
_____
_____
_____
_____
_____
_____

Just Write Bitch!

Think back to a special birthday from when you were younger. Describe as many specific details as you can, using each of your senses.

_____
_____
_____
_____
_____
_____
_____
_____
_____
_____
_____
_____
_____
_____
_____
_____
_____
_____
_____
_____
_____
_____
_____
_____
_____
_____
_____
_____

Just Write Bitch!

What is one thing you want more than anything else? How does that desire feel?

_____
_____
_____
_____
_____
_____
_____
_____
_____
_____
_____
_____
_____
_____
_____
_____
_____
_____
_____
_____
_____
_____
_____
_____
_____

Just Write Bitch!

Who are the people in your life that make you feel the most
at ease? What is it about them that makes you feel that way?

_____

_____

_____

_____

_____

_____

_____

_____

_____

_____

_____

_____

_____

_____

_____

_____

_____

_____

_____

_____

_____

_____

_____

_____

_____

_____

Just Write Bitch!

When was the last time you cried? What caused it?

_____
_____
_____
_____
_____
_____
_____
_____
_____
_____
_____
_____
_____
_____
_____
_____
_____
_____
_____
_____
_____
_____
_____
_____
_____
_____
_____

Just Write Bitch!

Write a letter of forgiveness to yourself.

_____
_____
_____
_____
_____
_____
_____
_____
_____
_____
_____
_____
_____
_____
_____
_____
_____
_____
_____
_____
_____
_____
_____
_____
_____

Just Write Bitch!

What was the last quasi-random thing that made you smile?
Where were you? Were you alone? What were you thinking?

Just Write Bitch!

What do you think is the worst thing you've ever done?

_____

_____

_____

_____

_____

_____

_____

_____

_____

_____

_____

_____

_____

_____

_____

_____

_____

_____

_____

_____

_____

_____

_____

_____

_____

_____

_____

Just Write Bitch!

What one place brings about the most positive memories for you? What does it look like, feel like, smell like?

_____
_____
_____
_____
_____
_____
_____
_____
_____
_____
_____
_____
_____
_____
_____
_____
_____
_____
_____
_____
_____
_____
_____
_____
_____
_____

Just Write Bitch!

What are your thoughts or beliefs about psychics, seers, intuitives? Are these your own or something you've inherited from someone else?

_____
_____
_____
_____
_____
_____
_____
_____
_____
_____
_____
_____
_____
_____
_____
_____
_____
_____
_____
_____
_____
_____
_____
_____
_____

Just Write Bitch!

What was the biggest lie you've ever told? Why?

_____
_____
_____
_____
_____
_____
_____
_____
_____
_____
_____
_____
_____
_____
_____
_____
_____
_____
_____
_____
_____
_____
_____
_____
_____
_____
_____
_____

Just Write Bitch!

What do you know about your parent's childhoods? How did
this shape your own childhood?

_____
_____
_____
_____
_____
_____
_____
_____
_____
_____
_____
_____
_____
_____
_____
_____
_____
_____
_____
_____
_____
_____
_____
_____
_____
_____

Just Write Bitch!

What are 10 things on your bucket list? If you don't already have a bucket list, now's a great time to start one!

_____
_____
_____
_____
_____
_____
_____
_____
_____
_____
_____
_____
_____
_____
_____
_____
_____
_____
_____
_____
_____
_____
_____
_____
_____
_____
_____
_____

Just Write Bitch!

What would your childhood self think of who you are today?

_____
_____
_____
_____
_____
_____
_____
_____
_____
_____
_____
_____
_____
_____
_____
_____
_____
_____
_____
_____
_____
_____
_____
_____
_____
_____
_____
_____

Just Write Bitch!

Imagine yourself as a superhero. What does your power suit look like? Spandex, fishnets, a cape, mask? What colors? How does it make you feel? And, most importantly, what's your superpower?

_____

_____

_____

_____

_____

_____

_____

_____

_____

_____

_____

_____

_____

_____

_____

_____

_____

_____

_____

_____

_____

_____

_____

_____

_____

_____

Just Write Bitch!

Does thinking about the future scare or excite you? Why?

_____
_____
_____
_____
_____
_____
_____
_____
_____
_____
_____
_____
_____
_____
_____
_____
_____
_____
_____
_____
_____
_____
_____
_____
_____

Just Write Bitch!

What is your philosophy on life? What do you see as being the meaning of life? Why? Where do you think this came from?

_____

_____

_____

_____

_____

_____

_____

_____

_____

_____

_____

_____

_____

_____

_____

_____

_____

_____

_____

_____

_____

_____

_____

_____

_____

_____

Just Write Bitch!

What are the 3 most important lessons you've learned in life so far? What experiences or situations taught you these lessons?

_____
_____
_____
_____
_____
_____
_____
_____
_____
_____
_____
_____
_____
_____
_____
_____
_____
_____
_____
_____
_____
_____
_____
_____
_____
_____
_____

Just Write Bitch!

Write about the last dream you can remember in as much detail as possible.

Just Write Bitch!

Think back to your childhood best friend. What would you like to tell them about your life now? Write them a letter, catching them up on what you've been doing for the last 20/30/40/50 years.

_____

_____

_____

_____

_____

_____

_____

_____

_____

_____

_____

_____

_____

_____

_____

_____

_____

_____

_____

_____

_____

_____

_____

_____

_____

Just Write Bitch!

If you were given the choice between seeing the future &
living forever, which would you choose & why?

_____
_____
_____
_____
_____
_____
_____
_____
_____
_____
_____
_____
_____
_____
_____
_____
_____
_____
_____
_____
_____
_____
_____
_____
_____

Just Write Bitch!

Describe a single significant life event that has helped shape
who you are today. Do you consider this to have been a
positive or negative thing?

_____
_____
_____
_____
_____
_____
_____
_____
_____
_____
_____
_____
_____
_____
_____
_____
_____
_____
_____
_____
_____
_____
_____
_____
_____
_____

Just Write Bitch!

What was your favorite toy or game as a child? What did you love most about it? Was it something you shared with others or kept to yourself?

_____

_____

_____

_____

_____

_____

_____

_____

_____

_____

_____

_____

_____

_____

_____

_____

_____

_____

_____

_____

_____

_____

_____

_____

_____

_____

_____

_____

Just Write Bitch!

What is one experience or story that you never want your
mother to read? Don't censor yourself!

_____

_____

_____

_____

_____

_____

_____

_____

_____

_____

_____

_____

_____

_____

_____

_____

_____

_____

_____

_____

_____

_____

_____

_____

_____

_____

_____

Just Write Bitch!

What are your thoughts on fate or destiny? Fact or fiction?
What experiences have developed this belief?

_____
_____
_____
_____
_____
_____
_____
_____
_____
_____
_____
_____
_____
_____
_____
_____
_____
_____
_____
_____
_____
_____
_____
_____
_____

Just Write Bitch!

What scares you? Why?

_____
_____
_____
_____
_____
_____
_____
_____
_____
_____
_____
_____
_____
_____
_____
_____
_____
_____
_____
_____
_____
_____
_____
_____
_____
_____
_____
_____

Just Write Bitch!

What was the last spontaneous thing you did? How did you feel?

_____
_____
_____
_____
_____
_____
_____
_____
_____
_____
_____
_____
_____
_____
_____
_____
_____
_____
_____
_____
_____
_____
_____
_____
_____
_____

Just Write Bitch!

What single event has most shaped who you are currently?
How?

_____

_____

_____

_____

_____

_____

_____

_____

_____

_____

_____

_____

_____

_____

_____

_____

_____

_____

_____

_____

_____

_____

_____

_____

_____

_____

_____

_____

_____

_____

Just Write Bitch!

What big hairy scary goals do you have for yourself this year? Why? What steps can you take today towards achieving them?

_____
_____
_____
_____
_____
_____
_____
_____
_____
_____
_____
_____
_____
_____
_____
_____
_____
_____
_____
_____
_____
_____
_____
_____
_____
_____

Just Write Bitch!

Imagine, you're on your deathbed with only moments left to live, what confessions would you make? To whom?

_____
_____
_____
_____
_____
_____
_____
_____
_____
_____
_____
_____
_____
_____
_____
_____
_____
_____
_____
_____
_____
_____
_____
_____
_____
_____

Just Write Bitch!

What is one of your earliest memories? Describe it in as much detail as possible.

_____

_____

_____

_____

_____

_____

_____

_____

_____

_____

_____

_____

_____

_____

_____

_____

_____

_____

_____

_____

_____

_____

_____

_____

_____

_____

_____

Just Write Bitch!

Do you believe in soul mates? Why or why not?

_____
_____
_____
_____
_____
_____
_____
_____
_____
_____
_____
_____
_____
_____
_____
_____
_____
_____
_____
_____
_____
_____
_____
_____
_____
_____

Just Write Bitch!

What are 3 questions you'd like to ask an older version of yourself, now?

_____

_____

_____

_____

_____

_____

_____

_____

_____

_____

_____

_____

_____

_____

_____

_____

_____

_____

_____

_____

_____

_____

_____

_____

_____

_____

Just Write Bitch!

What fears did you have as a child? Were they real or imagined?

_____
_____
_____
_____
_____
_____
_____
_____
_____
_____
_____
_____
_____
_____
_____
_____
_____
_____
_____
_____
_____
_____
_____
_____
_____
_____

Just Write Bitch!

What are 3 ordinary things within your daily life that bring you joy? What is it about these items? Were these gifts, found objects, or something else?

_____
_____
_____
_____
_____
_____
_____
_____
_____
_____
_____
_____
_____
_____
_____
_____
_____
_____
_____
_____
_____
_____
_____
_____
_____
_____

Just Write Bitch!

What are the 5 most memorable moments of your life so far? Why?

_____

_____

_____

_____

_____

_____

_____

_____

_____

_____

_____

_____

_____

_____

_____

_____

_____

_____

_____

_____

_____

_____

_____

_____

_____

_____

_____

Extra Pages